Enjoy!
Kellette Hale

The Poet Within

Penetrating the Depths

By

Kellette Gale

1663 LIBERTY DRIVE, SUITE 200
BLOOMINGTON, INDIANA 47403
(800) 839-8640
WWW.AUTHORHOUSE.COM

© 2005 Kellette Gale. All Rights Reserved.

No part of this book may be reproduced, stored in a retrieval system, or transmitted by any means without the written permission of the author.

First published by AuthorHouse 01/20/05

ISBN: 1-4208-2017-6 (sc)

Printed in the United States of America
Bloomington, Indiana

This book is printed on acid-free paper.

Dedication

This is a book about life, love and spirituality. It is about life because in reading this book, one might learn a few life lessons. It is about love because it was created from love and is a work that addresses the many aspects of love. This work is about spirituality because it is spiritually based and speaks of spirituality. These are the reasons for which I have decided to dedicate this book to the women of the world. Women seem to have it hard these days, especially the working woman. We have so many hats to wear and through it all we still seem to be the ones who love the deepest.

Women are the people who live an example of unconditional love daily. I witness this everyday amongst my family. So, to all the women out there...

> To the daughter, the sister
> The wonderful mother
> The wife, the aunt
> The courageous grandmother
> Be the child, the friend
> And the excellent role model
> The partner, the godmother
> And always remember to stay true to
> Yourself!

Acknowledgements

This work would not be possible without God. I would first like to thank him. I also give thanks to my family especially my immediate family for their undying patience and love.

Table of Contents

Dedication v
Acknowledgements vii
About the Author.. xi
Preface xv
Introduction xvii
Words...Unrevised 1
A True Blessing 3
Sign of the Times... 5
A Prayer 7
Him.. 9
Everything Living, God is Now 11
A Blessing in Disguise 13
Deep Apology 15
Chance Meeting 17
I Love 19
My Soul Mate... 21
Life and Death 23
Peace 25
Dreams 27
Untitled I.. 29
Real Man.. 31
Penetrating the Depths of Reality 33
Are You There...Hello...Do You Hear Me? 35
Beautiful One 37
Where Are You?... 39

Love Sonnet No. 4	41
Divine Steps to Happiness	43
Love at First Sight	45
I Received His Peace	47
Things Change	49
Deep in the Street	51
You	53
Woman	55
Love	57
Untitled II	59
Feeling	61
Letting Go	63
Untitled III	65
The Loving Him	67
A Dream of Love	69
New Baby	71
Passing On	73
With Patience, Good Things Come	75
Words II	77
Reach Within	79
Love is Forever	81
False Love	83
Discovering Your Inner Poet	85

About the Author

I am an artist
Poet, if you will
The brush is my intellect
The paint
The energy within my being
I shape its flow with my consciousness
And by the grace of God
I unleash
What it is that I call

GOODNESS!

I am single because
I am addicted
To the idea
Of forever
Afraid of never
Waiting for always
Emanating that virgo love
Looking for he who compliments me
In that special way that makes me say

"I LOVE YOU"

Kellette "Kellie" Gale is a native of the Washington D.C. Metropolitan area. She grew up in Temple Hills, Maryland along with her three sisters under the supervision of her mother and father. Kellie is a growing poet who loves to write and a true advocate of the pursuit of truth and oneness through the art of meditation. She is a graduate of Morgan State University's School of Natural Sciences. She graduated in the year 2000 as a Chemistry major.

Kellie is sure of her spiritual path of enlightenment that she consciously surrendered her life to not too long after the sudden death of her father, whom she continues to respect and love very truly.

Kellie's poetry emphasizes how important it is to love God and have faith in him. She also writes about self-discipline which she believes is an imperative virtue to have growing up in a society whose goals tend to stray away from the true order of God. She hopes to uplift and enlighten any soul who happens to come across her art.

Knowing who I am
Discovering why I am
And springing forth the person I am
Meant to be

Preface

In the midst of seen nothingness
There exists an observable sense of enchantment
From this mystical state of consciousness
There resides the ability to reach
Into the depths of intangible existence
Radiance surrounds this unseen entity
Allowing its slightest touch
To enlighten any soul who desires
To embark upon a somewhat difficult
Yet totally fulfilling
Path of illumination
When the student is ready
The teacher shall appear

Magically so, as if without warning
So blissful the experience
The child is left mourning
A feeling by providence
Fated to be
It is the exact circumstance needed
To lead one's destiny
Step by Step under God's beck and call
Individual consciousness of choice
Shall be the basis of one's all

Or so it is for me
I can feel nothing but Poetry
Bubbling out of me
Like a volcano ready to erupt
A flaming torch
Too powerful to disrupt

This energy-exploding affinity
Is undeniably approaching infinity
Enticing me with the beauty
Of eternity
It is from within me
That this magic of love
Seems to be
Flowing rather steadily
This motion sets me free
I must go there before I go anywhere
There is no time to spare
I must live for love in order to share.

Introduction

Divinity in the Making

Time and patience allow for creativity and wisdom
Creativity and wisdom allow for beauty and truth
Beauty and truth allow an open heart
An open heart awakens many a soul
An awakened soul reflects oneness with Christ

In time
the virtue of patience
enhances the creative flow of a being
enlightening one to wisdom
This beauty of truth
guides the way for an open heart
by awakening it's very soul
This awakened soul
blessed in many ways
touches yet another soul
In turn
an effect is put into motion
known as the Domino Effect
Each one, teach one, to reach one
Reflect Christ in your life
Always remember
patience is a dimension of time
Patience is a virtue

Words...Unrevised

There are words flying around the galaxy
Above the ethers for all to see
Upon interaction with the air
All breath makes sound for all to share
As oxygen penetrates each brain cell
We are able to form words without fail
So quickly, even hastily
We don't even think
How our words may affect others
How our sound may cause them to shrink
So meaningful our thought
So powerful its manifestation
It is important to think before speaking
In every situation
Our words have wings
And anyone may hear them
As words never die
They tend to fly away
Even go astray
Penetrating distant galaxies of stars
Understand your words will be heard
Your thoughts will be felt
Whether here or on mars
Our words vibrate
Much, much higher
Than even the wisest sire
That is –depending on
How clever the thought
That causes the sound
To form the word
Through the voice

It's your choice
Enter the dimension
Where all words reside
Although they may travel fast
There is no where for them to hide

A True Blessing

I'm in a different time
A new dimension
And I feel ecstasy when I think of you
A feeling no drug can put me through
I am happy with the thought of you
The thought that there is
Someone actually out there who
Understands me and loves
Me enough to want to be true
I am high on life knowing
That you feel the same way about me too
I am in awe of my own
Impression of you
Touched by all that you say and do
Swept away by the thoughts that we've shared
Wondering if you know how
Much I really care
I am in love with our compatibility
Knowing you makes me feel free
Your personality is so refreshing
Like no other, having you in my life feels
Like a true blessing

Sign of the Times

The sign of times
Is weighing heavy on my soul
My lot in life has proven
To be quite and expensive toll
"Looking for love in all the wrong places"
My truth from within is my only salvation
Alone, I try hard to breathe, as, so fast, my heart races
An understandable battle I am facing
From the beginning, my steps, I have been tracing
Looking forward to rest and relaxation
True oneness with God, eliminating all vexation
A whole person, ready for truth
Allowing for guidance, allowing for love
Allowing for wisdom from above

A Prayer

I pray for the day
Fruit springeth from my tree
Blossoms of love
Swinging so heavenly
In the wind
A resurrection
A testimonial to truth
Being all I can be
Seeing all there is to see
Understanding life as a whole
Becoming an independent soul
A truth seeker, I am
Walking through life
Fulfilling a purpose of connecting love
Truth is love
As it is above, so shall it be below
As it is within, so shall it be on out
Three dimensional awareness,
Becomes patient in the fourth
Time, an infinite dimension
Extending its hands to that of peace
Within is where church begins
Infinite oneness with God
True happiness
Living with God
Hearing his word
Becoming his word.
The truth,
Christ Consciousness

Him

When I met him
He touched me
When I saw him
He kissed me
When I left him
He hugged me
When he left me
I cried

When I spoke to him
He listened
When I laughed he smiled
When I touched him
He tingled
When I trusted him
He lied

Everything Living, God is Now

The only man that acknowledges my heart
The only man that is patient enough to understand
He sees my spirit and loves it
He truly represents a real man
For me, no one could ever see me
Let alone take the time to glance
Into my spirit that yearns,
Into my heart
That starves for romance
Such a lonely life I lead
Dodging false love and negativity
Even at top notch speed,
I find it difficult to live respectfully
I love myself and all I have to give
Now, if only my true love
Could find a similar interest
For which to live
Am I to blame
For my mind's wandering bout
Entertaining angels unaware,
Admiring their character of stout
I am sorry for the comfort I receive from another
    Man's heart
For I withstand silent tears
Hoping it won't tear us apart
My experiences of lust
Never last forever
They are merely moments of weakness, somehow,
    Passing the time until we are together
Because even after the blessings of the night
My soul, still, cries from within

Looking for a brighter tomorrow
Looking for a more familiar sight

A Blessing in Disguise

Oh, to be blessed
By a true Karmic Test
When all that is going wrong
Doesn't want to end
And God no longer seems
To be your very best friend
Stop and take the time
To reach within

The disguise this tragedy bears
Really isn't all that clever
Here is your chance to show your stuff
And grab hold of the treasure

Verily and carefully
Gather all of your virtue
That is –innocence, endurance,
Prophetic vision too
Patience, stability, versatility, sensitivity
Courage, nobility, generosity, honesty
Compassion, justice, wisdom and even further
Love, light, truth and order

Stand tall, be strong
Because there is nothing really wrong
God is watching you grab hold of the ember
Giving you yet another chance to finally remember

Deep Apology

Be I guilty for opening my door?
Or be you guilty for opening yours?
Words we have exchanged
And friends we will remain
The past was a gift
As precious as this present
I give to you my love
Though intangible, very valuable
For it is, you see
Delivered only through me
And still, respect I demand
For without it, I am not a woman
And you, not a man
Allow me to restore our dignity
And offer my apologies to you
In honor of him
But as I give, I do believe
I too am worthy to receive
With this I beg
Please be kind
As is said
To err is human, to forgive, divine
And one by one we shall pick up the pieces
And slowly remember our role
Brought here to fulfill a goal
As God governs the soul
The strength of our individual characters
In all its goodness will prevail
This journey we have traveled
Together set sail
Thoughts of inspirations

Feelings of elation
Even great expectations
To now only be regarded as memory
Whether good or bad in your eyes
God sees fit to ensure me, of its positivity
You have brought you see
Much insight to me
Much love, much wisdom
In all its glory
Much spice to my life
And no worry
Through the mere possibility
That you and me could become ...ONE!

Chance Meeting

It was by chance that I sought him
It was by chance that I met him
Only to find myself in awe
Inspired by his beautiful character
I sought out to know more
Who is this person who has undeniably
Caught my attention...with his heart?

He is ... so cool!

                He is ... so open!

                                He is...so wise!

WOW!

He's loving, caring, nurturing, and inspiring
He has opened my heart to new feelings
And I am happy.

I am happy to know such a wonderful man.

I Love

I love much
Many people I love
Secretly
There is no real measure
Of how or why
Or when or even if I try
To love so deeply
Within my heart
It is true to me
To be
In love
With you
Yesterday, I loved truly
When I spoke to you from my heart
Secretly
I love
Never did I say that forbidden word
Never did I say I and you to you
With it in between
I love deeply
I love mainly he but she receives it too
Secretly I love
Secretly love
I'm sure you too do

My Soul Mate

I believe in you
Just as I believe in me
I believe that we were meant to be
Every obstacle in my life
Only brings me closer to being
Your most perfect wife
Every man in my life
Displays pieces of you
To become whole in you
When I meet you
Every day I dream of that glorious night
When our eyes meet
And our souls reunite

I dream of love at night
Together
Me and you
Under the moonlight
Gazing in each other's eyes
Enjoying the starry skies
My heart beats to your presence
Your spirit over takes my essence

Life and Death

Life
At its best
Is an endless road of miracles
Tending to ignite sparks of passion
At just the right moments
There is love
Tempering despair
Growing knowledge
Understanding each other
Remembering truth
Seeing God
Life

Death
A mere illusion
To die in life is to die in death
For on earth
Life is death
And death leaves this life ongoing
With God
God is truth
Consciousness is life
Where there is life
There is no death
Where there is God
There is no death
God is life
Live in God
And you will live forever
With Him in all happiness

Peace

Peace to all that is real
I am one of the elite
In my own space
And in my own time
I represent
The child within
The beauty that begins
The mystery
When I speak
The blessings roll off my tongue
Expressing deep inspiring words of forever
Together
With Christ on my side
I take the stride
Of a lifetime
As I extract thought and deliver
My river runs deep
Barely touching the shore
For sure
I am that which God has made me to be
Conquering all obstacles that claim me
Nothing can break that which cannot be broken
Inside, I am strong
And I long for the day
Eternity comes my way
And I stand at the gate
And wait
For He
Him
In all his essence
Yes I live for that day
I witness his presence

Dreams

Dreams have a way of flowing through
Your body and sending you to a familiar place
A place you know you have been before
But can not exactly recall when
That is why
Dreams should be held close to your heart
Because it is your intuition guiding your thoughts
Sometimes they may seem confusing
While at other times they are quite clear
But this is only a way of reminding your mind
Of your soul which has already been here
You are your soul and your soul knows everything
It needs to lead you up that big rainbow road
Toward that great big pot of gold
Our brain has been reprogrammed by time
To believe everything we see
But it's our intuition that reminds us that
A tree is not a tree
But how could this be?
It is truth
A tree is not a tree
A tree is free
To grow and blow with the wind
It is merely here to help us along the way
To remind us that behind all material manifestations
Hides the truth
A deeper knowing of what is
What was,
And what will be
Follow your heart and you will see

Untitled I

You are more than can be said
Inspiration beyond time
The love which
Does which
To guide my mind
Body
And soul
You are that which is needed to mold
You represent centuries of forgotten gold
You got me feeling it all
Your compassionate fury
Your sincere thoughts of purity
You speak from your heart
And definitely play the part
You are that which does which
Needs to be done for all
Straight forward and direct
Deserving nothing but my respect
My loves goes out to you
A soldier, a warrior, a king of supreme goodness
That angry lover
Has recovered
The spirituality
And sensuality
We all must discover
To be uncovered in due time
He who sees the divine
And works within the miracles of the spine
You are a computer genius, web master extraordinaire
You fit the bill and are...

REAL!

Real Man

I can truly appreciate an intelligent black man
No matter what your age
You have the power to stop the rage
That upsets the black community
For if you touch only one
Your job has just begun

PEACE MAN!

Find it within yourself
To discover the truth about wealth
It lies not within your material accumulations
But yes, in your spiritual dedications

ONE LOVE!

Believe in yourself, Believe in God
Love yourself, Love God
Complete the circle and become whole
Because that is what I call being real to your soul

Penetrating the Depths of Reality

I produce my own lyrics
I write my own song
This flow I pour
Is more steady than ever before
Igniting a fire
Selecting ears for hire
To hear the story of old
Coming through like gold
Reminding all souls
Of the divine goals
That put us here in the beginning
The truth was never lost
We just started sinning
The flow remained
The couple stayed
The cycle of life
Promises no fade
Of the truth
For it's always there
We share the commonality
Of spiritual immortality
To be invoked upon desire
It's our thoughts that take us higher
And higher past the sky there is no limit
The fault is yours if you forget
The power that is in it
Empowers you with the ability to win it
ALL
Fail is only relative when time is considered
And even then who cares
Because the path is straight

The circle is complete
In the end the crown will be won
By no defeat

Are You There...Hello...Do You Hear Me?

Somewhere there is an angel
Overcome by the world's anger
Distraught by the world's sadness
Wanting to make a difference
Needing to make a change
Asking what needs to be done
Looking for the answer
Beginning with oneself
Striving to do what is right
Talking to God
Listening to God
Accepting God
Knowing God
Following God
Walking with God
Trusting in Him
Understanding his truth
Spreading his word
Leading by example

AMEN

Beautiful One

Such a beautiful man with an innocent heart
It is a shame that we must be torn apart
Your eyes are like one of a kind
It is as if diamonds are shining
Through the darkness it's behind
Amazingly beautiful
Is how you appear to me
I see nothing but your spark
Shining so exuberantly
Your smile is full of nothing but love
Your freedom is not unlike a baby dove
You seem to spark some peace within me
You have touched a place I thought
No one should be
It is too bad others must play with your heart
Confusing you while tearing us apart
I am aware of all of the hate
That you have been through
I understand how hard
It is to forget too
I am able to see your heartache
And feel your pain
This is how I know my love for you
Is not in vain
So big, so strong
Yet innocent like a child
Also small, never weak
Emotions running wild
Never let your anger get the best of you
Your experiences somehow
Show the you that is true

Where Are You?

I know you are standing here with me
But I can not see you
You are beautiful
I remember your essence
It lies within your choice
The past has bought you here
This present will take you
Where you choose to go
Nowhere else
Look forward to freedom
Learn from your mistakes
Make way for a brighter you
A more pleasant you
A wiser you
The true you
I miss you
And look forward to
Once again witnessing
Your essence

Love Sonnet No. 4

The truth that remains within my heart
Is the knowledge my soul tries to impart
Giddee up, Giddee up
My flow is just beginning
I am learning to truly love myself
And stop all of the sinning
Seclusion of myself from everyone around
Keeps my mind clear and straight
Nice and sound
I am on a mission
To teach and learn
Picking only the best
Applying love to discern
The feelings that I get
The moves that I make
Are divine by nature
By no mistake
I know what I feel
I feel what I know
My heart is the only one
Running this show

Divine Steps to Happiness

For every single soul
Who decided to take this earthly stroll
Everything in life happens for a divine reason
Even the "so-called" sad winter season
Although your decisions may seem to be made in vain
Ultimately causing you headache and mental strain
There is always a lesson waiting to be learned
So powerful it is and so worth being earned
God is behind you every step of the way
Guiding you to make sure you don't go astray
There is no flaw in your predestined life path
So just continue to follow God and you will avoid the wrath
Stay true, Stay humble...and don't distress
Infinite patience and unconditional love
Will spark your inner peace and put your mind at rest
Right knowledge and wisdom may make you feel strange
Just breathe deep through your nose and don't be afraid of change
No need to worry about what others think of you
Because God is on your side, especially when you stay true
"Observe with coupe" and become a witness
If you don't cause the drama, your opportunities will be endless
Your spirit will shine, your aura will glow
Not only will you feel the difference, but also
Your positive attitude will show
Your increasing faith in God, will be so pleasant and nice
It is the perfect ingredient, just the right spice
Get rid of your vices and round up all of your virtue
False pride and arrogance will only hurt you
I know it's not easy and will take some time

Just remember courage and innocence
And you will be just fine
You are yourself and have nothing to prove
Doing right under God, is just the right move

*dedicated to and inspired by one strong brother

Love at First Sight

Your eyes have proven to be my personal safe haven
For no other person knows the comfort they bring me
Contact simply melts my heart
Opening my eyes to you
A bridge whose existence is held only by our love
Slightly embraces me
It is enough to stop time
I see nothing but your face
So beautifully put together
I feel nothing but your love
Its warmth excites me
I smell nothing but your breath
As sweet as can be
I hear nothing but your sound
Your silent messages overtake me
As mysterious as night
Yet as clear as day
This love that I felt before
Has reminded me of my way
Lost in life with no certain of truth
Lack of love and guidance left me aloof
Spiritually unaware of even myself
No knowledge, No power
No fulfilling wealth
God's name was the wisdom I had to back me
I remained a believer though uncertain of his identity
He answered my prayers and showed me your face
Now I am at peace and out of the race
Memories of love lasting forever
Deep feelings we had
When last we were together

Your eyes reveal to me your heart and your soul
A portrait of beauty
That helps me become whole

I Received His Peace

Ever so lovingly
I received his peace
And had to know
What beckoned him to release
Such a wonderful gesture
Under no pressure
Which I received with my heart
But just as fast as he appeared
He began to depart
My curiosity grew
In patience I waited
Putting together every clue
And after moments of confusion
That were never ever true
I finally deciphered the puzzle
And once again knew
The purpose of my life
He so clearly imparted
With every single word
Every sentence he started
He revealed to me, unguarded
Pieces of my very own soul
What a wonderful man
Playing such a beautiful role
He has touched my heart
And opened my life
Helping me to understand love
And forget all strife
He awakened my passion
Helping me to grow
Giving me the strength of mind

And the courage to know
The truth of myself
And everyone else

Things Change

It's funny how situations change
If your time and position isn't right
You begin to rearrange
Subconscious thoughts ponder your head
Of the way thing used to be
Should be and are
How your word isn't enough evidence
To mark what you said
And when it comes down to the book
Surprisingly your page is the one being read
You thought your brain was so sharp
Like some d-a-m-n pencil lead
When the truth remains
It isn't even up to par
When being compared
To the ever flowing universal law
Finally
Back to reality
It is your turn to gain truth
It is time to forget about what has been done
Enough is enough
Let us just learn the lesson

Deep in the Street

Deep in the street
Buckled tightly in his seat
Of innocent ignorance
Blind to consequence
Spiritually oppressed
Intellectually suppressed
Wearily distressed
It is true that the barriers they build
And the lies they told
Only make us more powerful
And all the more bold
A man with no vision
May lead you to a cliff
Just listen to God
Whose purpose is to uplift
You will see
Your spirit shall call
And the blind man shall fall
The ideas satan speaks
Isn't even worth a look
Our purpose and our plan
Resides in the good book
How hard can it be
To stand up and be free
Let us rebuke material gain
And forget about it with no shame
"better a poor man, strong and robust,
than a rich man with wasted frame"
                -Sirach 30:14

You

If I could hear the melody
that soothes your flow
If I could taste the spices
      That caress your tongue
If I could see the vision
      That guides your way

I would feel blessed to know
      That I have shared a piece of you
That makes me want to stay

...enticed by your beauty
      and mesmerized by your love
          the essence of you
has touched me from above

Woman

It is your inspiration that helps me keep moving
Sounding so soothing
Your wisdom becomes something for me to live by
You have raised many a child
To become wonderful human beings
You have taught me lessons of unconditional love
I have learned so much from you
And I thank God for allowing me to know
Such wonderful and beautifully strong beings
You are definitely a divine work of his art
And your role is more than just a part
You display, to me,
Wholeness and oneness with God
Strength of eternity
Knowledge of truth
Blessings of forever
I am surrounded by your beauty
And I pray that within yourself
You are feeling what I am saying
You are special
And must be treated that way

Love

Love

Love is that feeling of wanting to do better
That knowledge of truth and guidance from above
Love is the beauty of friendship

Love is unconditional feelings of happiness, sacrifice,
And oneness with God

Love is intimacy, warmth, kindness, generosity
Loyalty, peace and strength of character

When I think of love,

I think of joyfulness, earnestness, togetherness and family

Caring and sharing

Love is feeling oneness with each other for a special
moment of interconnectedness

Love is ongoing
Love is forever
Love is patient
Love is faith

Love

Untitled II

The way you express feeling
Is a good way of healing
Yourself
And others around you
It is true
That
What we say
When we pray
Are testimonials to truth
That gives us
Ideas and clues
About what is right
Understanding God's will
Takes only the desire to know
And then to do so
Coming up in today's society
Requires that you be patient
And awaken that which is latent
Within you
Your inner spirit
Your inner poet
Your inner notion
That something needs to be done
It is up to you to discover
That which needs to be uncovered
For your own good
Let us be smart in our neighborhoods

Feeling

You are such a beautiful person
Your thoughts inspire my every blessing
Your words send tremors through my body
Keeping me wanting for more
You are so refreshing
Thank you for touching me
I feel your energy as it flows
And I know I want to be with you
When we are standing together
Embracing each other and touching
I squeeze you so tight
And wonder inside, "How can I get closer?"

Letting Go

When I loved him
He loved me
When I was there for him
He used me
When I left him
He cried for me
When He left me
I survived the heartache
Of losing a love
We shared good times
And bad times
When he wouldn't let me leave
I felt irritated because
He didn't know how to tell me
When I didn't want him to leave
I watched him walk away
As my heart began to feel empty
Without him
I never cried
But instead
I knew in my heart that this was best
He never once turned back
He just faded off in the distance
A friend, a lover, an intelligent man
Who made me happy for so long
We were young and exuberant
Independent souls who
Met, loved, separated and still,
I love

Untitled III

Drip Drop
      Drip Drop
Each one as delicate as the first

Drip Drop
      Drip Drop
Each one as strong as the last

One by one
      We come
Into existence
As young souls
So bold, yet so old
Remembering events of a past
Holding on to a vision of a future
Loving one God
Who strengthens us from within
Learning old lessons
Remembering old songs
Forgotten in the wave of time

We are the past
We are the present
We are the future

We come together as one
To form true consciousness
Within our being
Enlightening ourselves to wisdom
Opening the doors to knowledge
Little by little

Taking one step closer
Day by day
To that special place
We long to remember
When that day comes

Oh Grace!

We will dance in
Heavenly oneness with God
And with each other in all
Goodness!

The Loving Him

When I met him
I immediately fell in love
His silly ways was nothing
More than his youth shining through
He knew about love
And loved much

I witnessed his love

His love of women
His love of God
His love of himself

His love spoke to me

In a special way

A soul mate
A king

My heart opens at the thought of him
Nestled within himself
So comfortable with himself
Loving all
Understanding much
And living it
Living a life of dedication
Striving to do what is best
Sharing happiness

A Dream of Love

I am looking to the stars
And heavens above
To secure my dreams
Of finding love
From within me
I am yearning
My heart is full
And my mind is burning
Burning with excitement
Of yet another day
To look for he who compliments
My beautiful way
I smile up at God
For he is the one
Who keeps me going
And wanting to have fun
That day will come
And I will seize it
I am alive
And ready to receive it
My father is present
And reminds me of that special thing
I have inside me
That makes my heart sing
I follow my every blessing
To that dear place
A place that's full
Of nothing but God's good grace
While I await that special someone
God is with me
Ensuring he will come

He may be disguised
But I'll know he is the one
The occurrence will be
Nothing short of a miracle
Our eyes will meet
The situation will be mystical
Our story will be that of happiness
As it will be the start
Of our life together
We'll never be apart

New Baby

Baby's coming
And mom's excited!
She's getting ready
Her mind is delighted
With many ideas
Of what to do
Daddy's there
To help her through
Bibs, clothes
And other items
Wonderful ways
To continue to excite them
Friends and loved ones
Give their best wishes
Mom and dad
Are flooded with kisses
All for baby
Who is on the way
What a wonderful blessing
To receive today

Passing On

God has been waiting
To bring you home
To see the loved ones
Who left you alone
With family and friends
Who hold you dear
We wish you could have stayed
Forever here

Remembered friends and relatives
I'm sure are excited
They're ready to see you
Be so delighted
With a welcoming home
You are sure to love
This moment was planned
In heaven above

We'll miss you dear loved one
And your loving ways
We'll celebrate your life
For many days
But we love you for leaving
And guiding the way
To a new life with God
With whom we'll all stay

With Patience, Good Things Come

The love you show to me
Is beautifully kind
Your words are exquisite
Your thoughts are divine

I feel our spirits linked
By an unforeseen line
I see your every blessing
And I want to make you mine

I have been in love before
And although it was fun
When I got to know the man behind the muscle
His anger burned
Like the sun

I feel you must be different
You've already shown me
With your speech
When I think of you
I think of love
And I hope that's not
Beyond our reach

I want this to be special
Something we both can enjoy
But I think it's important we move slow
To avoid any chance of a ploy

When I think about what's best
My thoughts say we should wait
Let's be intimate later
Patient now
That way,
We can build something great

Words II

Your words are more powerful than you know
The blows send shocks through my soul
As I think to retaliate
I think again because I don't need that on my plate
Karma goes along way
And it can start with what you say
But when you bring it my way
You might as well step outside
Because I don't play
I will close the door behind you
And go my separate way
I'll tell you to stay out of my life
With all that petty mess
Or learn how to speak to me with respectfulness
I deserve it, and so do you
When you hear me say this
I know you know it's true
Take heed and try to understand
You can do it, I know you can
I care for you as I do myself
And I hope I am not saying this for my health
But when it comes to your words
And even the energy you put behind them
It tends to be the negative slurs
That I find disturbing with every whim
Just as you can make one happy
Another may get hurt
How do you feel when someone
Has made you alert
Eyes all big with shock, trying to think of a reply
Now is that the way you want things to be

Us going back and forth
Like we
Don't love
Let's be nicer to each other
Let's act like we care
Not only about our own
But each other's welfare

Reach Within

Look deep within yourself
To reveal to you….the truth
And nothing else
It's like when you look to the skies
And communicate
With that which lies
Many millions of miles away
Embrace that beauty
That you encounter
Keep that good feeling
As your spirit opens
And becomes one with the universe
Your energy is uplifted
And you discover
The most beautiful gift of all
Is that which you share with others
Take time to recover
The power which is held within
The power to understand and the power to know
The power to discern with your heart
And the power to grow
The power to love and the power to dream
The power of revealing that this world
Is not like it seems
Hold fast to the miracles that come your way
Create them with your mind and with what you say
Believe in what is real and give thanks to God
For he is beside you, protecting you, like a pea in a pod

Love is Forever

They say that love is forever
But our love see
Can't be
You keep telling me this
And telling me that
And all these things see
Are false to me
Because what you say
Never adds up
And love you see
Is supposed to add up
It's supposed to overflow my cup
But you and me
That is we
Never overflow
We just stay on the low
And yes, we do enjoy we
But afterwards
It's just me
I keep telling myself
He'll do better and
Maybe that crooked truth
Is a little straight
I mean, if I tilt my head
And close one eye
No.
Because for me to believe
What you say
I would have to be high
And that's only me
When I'm with me

Not with you because
What we have is so not true
So, go ahead
Keep telling those lies
But me, I'm not listening anymore
I'll be OK
Without you on my plate
My patience is strong
And for real love...
I can wait

False Love

Wined and dined, chakras all aligned
I'm surprised to see you here with me
But that's your specialty
To create an image in my mind
then present something different right on time
I'm ready to hear you be real with me
I'm ready to be alive and share with you
the idea of being free
looking into your eyes and seeing your soul
you're just the right size so big and so bold
I understand your every wish
I want to be with you to share a special kiss
Stay with me and flow with me
and be the one to grow with me
enlighten me and love me and be there for me
as I see the love in you I love your eyes
beautiful and full
shining at me I can't help but pull
you near to engulf what I feel
let's make this real

As I cuddle you and make you mine
Your eyes look away and you are appearing to be blind
you don't see me the way I see you
What a blow to the dream of us two
Why it can't happen now I see
I guess because we're different
and you don't really love me
You just want to use me for your selfish gain
another notch on the bed post
what a shame

To try to live like a player
when you know you're wrong
playing with my feelings
but just I'm too strong
To let that bother me at this point in my life
I'm moving on surpassing the strife
I'll know for next time when another one like you
shows his face to me, he'll turn blue
and be sad over me
the one who never turned her head
or took the time to see
what it could be
what it might become
I am no longer your play toy
That life is dumb
I'll be ok knowing I was right
He's just a player, he has no fight
of what it takes to know what's good
He just wants sex, His mentality is fake
I wish he'd grow up, for goodness's sake

Discovering Your Inner Poet
A Look into the Author's Personal Views

Writing can be a very exhilarating art in which to take part. Not only does it enhance your thinking skills, but also it allows you to express yourself in a personal manner. The works you create can be shared only if you, the author, feel comfortable enough to do so.

When you write, your words are special. Your thoughts become great expressions that allow you to reach others in profound ways. You become one with yourself as the process somehow allows you to reach deep for knowledge and truth. When you bring that out with your pen, you allow yourself to begin a cleansing process. This cleansing process begins with your mind and works its way throughout the rest of your body. In this way, you are opening your door to your inner poet.

Your inner poet or poet within can be discovered through many ways. For me, my poet within becomes active usually when I am alone. I could be driving my car listening to my inner radio, content with myself, and this is a time when my inner poet comes out.

Other times such as when I am listening to music, I may be inspired by the words I hear or maybe even the melody. But it is not until I am in a deep state of meditation that I really begin to understand myself and often meet my true poet within.

Discovering your poet within can be a wonderful experience. When I first discovered my poet within, I was shocked that the poetry was actually coming from inside of me. It was surprising for me to believe that I could come up with such wonderful words of wisdom.

My first poem dates back to 1986. I was just nine years of age and in the fourth grade. I remember needing to be able to write poetry. It was so beautiful to me and I wanted to create some. I remember my first poem.

My T.V.

My T.V. is so good
I saw E.T. and Red Riding Hood
I saw Golden Girls
And one bought some pearls
Now I'm watching 227
And it's only ten to eleven

I couldn't think of anything to write about. So, I decided to write about my T.V. I guess that was something important to me at that time. I was so proud of my first poem that I decided to write other poems. I ended up writing about three poems. Along with my sister Candace's two poems, we were good to go. We made a small poetry book and sold copies to other children for fifty cents each.

It wasn't until I was a junior in college that I truly found my true poet within. I was able to let go and let God. In doing so, I was also able to write about deep feelings that I held close to my heart. I will never forget that day. The poem I wrote became titled, "Divine Steps to Happiness". I feel that it is the most powerful thing I have ever written. I know it came from God. I believe that your true poet within is merely a connection your inner self has with God. Reaching your poet within is a true miracle...and miracles never cease.

Open your heart to wisdom
Embrace your soul of eternity
And recite this mantra

All you have to do is say yes!

YES!